ADIRONDACK EXPERIENCE

The Museum on Blue Mountain Lake

Adirondack Experience
in association with Scala Arts Publishers, Inc.

SCAL

Text and photography © 2019
Adirondack Experience:
The Museum on Blue Mountain Lake

Book © 2019
Scala Arts Publishers, Inc.

First published in 2019 by
Scala Arts Publishers, Inc.
c/o CohnReznick LLP
1301 Avenue of the Americas, 10th floor
New York, NY 10019
www.scalapublishers.com
Scala – New York – London

Distributed outside of
Adirondack Experience:
The Museum on Blue Mountain Lake
in the book trade by
ACC Art Books
6 West 18th Street
Suite 4B
New York, NY 10011

ISBN: 978-1-78551-190-5
Library of Congress Cataloging in
Publication Data: A catalogue record for
this book is available from the publisher.

Chief Curator at the Adirondack Experience:
Laura Rice

Edited by Eugenia Bell

Designed by Diane Gottardi

Printed in China
10 9 8 7 6 5 4 3 2 1

Front cover: Nancie Battaglia, Reflection of Blue
Mountain in Blue Mountain Lake, from the west.
Frontispiece: Nancie Battaglia, Blue Mountain Lake.
Above: Doreen Alessi, On Gothics looking toward
Mt. Marcy and the Upper Great Range, 2015.
Back cover: Water Witch, 1900.
Dividers: pp. 4–5, Life in the Adirondacks and
pond; pp. 34–35, Gary Randorf, East Hill, Keene,
1977; pp. 42–43: Breaking a jam, St. Regis River,
c. 1890; pp. 48–49, Rowing on Minnow Pond;
pp. 54–55, Seneca Ray Stoddard, Blue Mountain
House (Merwin's), c. 1880.

CONTENTS

Since opening its doors to the public in 1957, the Adirondack Experience has delighted millions of its visitors with fascinating exhibitions about life in the Adirondack region.

At times, the six-million acre Adirondack Park can be a challenging subject to document and explore. Unlike the great national parks, this park is a highly unusual mix of both public and private land. As a result, the desire to preserve and protect the landscape in pristine condition has often been at loggerheads with local residents' very real need to make a living in their own backyards. Located at the geographic center of the park, the **Adirondack Experience** is uniquely qualified to explore this fascinating dynamic and the stories of the people who have lived, worked, and played in the Adirondacks. The museum's unique collections document the full range of people's experiences from prehistory to the present day. The museum's paintings, photographs, boats, industrial equipment, manuscripts, books, motion picture films, and other materials provide the building blocks for engaging exhibitions that document the relationship between people and the landscape — and how that relationship has shaped a distinct regional identity that encompasses daily life, culture, and work.

The **Adirondack Experience's** exhibitions are displayed in twenty-three historic and contemporary buildings on 121 acres overlooking one of the Adirondack's natural wonders, Blue Mountain Lake. The exhibitions touch on varied topics from boating on Adirondack waters to logging to the artistry of Adirondack rustic furniture. The largest exhibition, *Life in the Adirondacks*, makes use of the latest in interactive techniques to immerse visitors in the reasons why we value nature and the deep attachments we form with it while honoring the people who have built the community and who are shaping the future of this place that we all love.

< Adirondack Museum on
Blue Mountain Lake, c. 1960.

—David M. Kahn, Executive Director

Jacques-Gerard Milbert, *Extremite de la Chutes D'Adley's* (Hadley's Falls), 1828–29, lithograph.

INTRODUCTION

When the first Europeans—soldiers, entrepreneurs, settlers—ventured into the Adirondack Mountains, they found a place unlike any other: a place of crystalline waters and sweet air, pristine forests and clear, luminous light. Artists were among the first to discover the region as well, bushwhacking through dense forests and enduring the constant annoyance of blackflies to create the first views Americans had of this wild landscape.

It was not, however, an uninhabited place, a pure wilderness. Native peoples lived in these mountains long before Europeans arrived. This region was, and remains, home to Mohawk and Abenaki peoples, whose history here stretches back millennia.

Snowshoes, c. 1890.

The Adirondack Mountains are rich in minerals and ores and abundant with timber. Exploitation of these natural resources during the nineteenth century brought more people and settlement and significantly changed the landscape. Concerns about widespread deforestation resulted in the establishment of the Forest Preserve in 1885 and, ultimately, the creation of the Adirondack Park in 1892.

Arthur Fitzwilliam Tait, *Autumn Morning*, 1872, oil on canvas.

Marion River Carry Pavilion and pond.

Today, the Adirondack Park is a six-million-acre patchwork of public and private land; the largest publicly protected area in the contiguous United States. Its borders are traditionally outlined in blue on official state maps. The acreage of Yellowstone, Glacier, Everglades, and the Grand Canyon National Parks would all fit inside the "Blue Line" with room to spare.

The Adirondack Mountains are laced with 3,000 lakes and ponds, 30,000 miles of rivers and streams, and some 2,000 miles of hiking trails: it is a mecca for outdoor sports enthusiasts. It is also a place in which many people come to connect with nature and self and find peace, inspiration, rejuvenation, and, for a happy few, home.

The **Adirondack Experience** stands at the geographic center of the Park. Since 1957, the museum's mission has been to share the stories of the people who have lived, worked, and played here: the **Adirondack Experience** expands public understanding of Adirondack history and the relationship between people and the Adirondack wilderness, fostering informed choices for the future.

Garnet Hill Lodge, North River, NY.

LIFE IN THE ADIRONDACKS

"Come with me up into a high mountain! Over a rippling ocean of forests first, their long swelling waves, now rising, now sinking down into deep hollows, here in grand mountains, crested as with caps of foam... the rude laugh is hushed... the body sinks down... the soul expands." —Photographer, cartographer, and guidebook writer Seneca Ray Stoddard, 1874

Gary Randorf, *Twin Pond, Dix Wilderness*, 1975.

The Adirondack Mountains have attracted people for millennia. There is something about this landscape, the quality of air and light, and the vast stretches of unbroken forest that appeals directly to the soul. We come to live, work, and play here, to renew ourselves, to heal, to feel grounded, to get away from our too-busy everyday lives. The Adirondacks change us—and we, in turn, have shaped the Adirondacks.

Our starting point is *Life in the Adirondacks*, a 19,000-square-foot exhibition that introduces the people and places, past and present, of the Adirondack Park and our evolving relationship with wilderness. We invite you to explore the museum's many other buildings and outdoor exhibits as well, for a closer view of the Adirondacks as home, work, play, and inspiration.

< Museum theater.

WILDERNESS STORIES

Whether a first-time visitor or a year-round resident, we each have our own wilderness story. The lure of the Adirondack Mountains is undeniable. For Ed Kanze, naturalist and Adirondack guide, it's an attachment that goes back for generations, rooted in family history: "A long connection to a place is mysterious, and I don't really believe I have it all figured out. But one thing I can say is that everywhere I go in this park, I'm going places where my ancestors walked. There's a connection here between people I'm related to that I've never known but I wish I could have, and they roamed these same landscapes that I roam today and that my kids explore, and I hope my grandchildren and beyond will explore here."

Naturalist Ed Kanze leading a tour on the Minnow Pond Trail.

That connection runs deep as well for Deb Osterhoudt and her family, an attachment that stems from their experiences climbing the forty-six High Peaks: "Being in the mountains, you know it becomes more a part of you. Instead of being in awe of them, it's more almost like who you are. Where at first you're just overcome by it, now you're part of it. We've hiked in the Green Mountains, the White Mountains, and we've hiked down south and we always come back. It's just, these mountains, they hold your heart ... they're not like anything else. They just aren't."

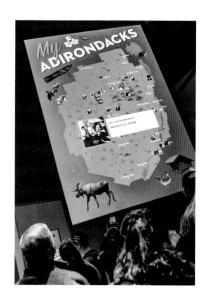

From Noonmark, High Peaks region. >

8

"**Few fully understand what the Adirondack wilderness really is.**
It is a mystery even to those who have crossed and recrossed it by boats along
its avenues, the lakes; and on foot through its vast and silent recesses...

—Verplanck Colvin, c. 1868

CALL OF THE WILDERNESS

Those of us answering the call of the Adirondack wilderness have arrived at different times and in different ways. We have come by railroad, steamboat, airplane, stagecoach, automobile, and on foot: miners and sportsmen, artists and entrepreneurs, tourists and athletes, rich and poor. We have come for different reasons, seeking wealth and health, fun and inspiration. Indigenous peoples have been here for thousands of years, and have always called this place home. More recent arrivals include French Canadian, Irish, English, Italian, Scandinavian, Lebanese, African American. You, too, are part of this community of seekers, whether you are here for a short visit or live here year-round.

Seneca Ray Stoddard, *"Goodbye"*
Adirondack Stage, 1872.

10

Verplanck Colvin, c. 1880.

The first Europeans to see the Adirondack landscape came to explore, to document military operations and fortifications, or to create maps and scientifically accurate images of the terrain, flora, and fauna.

Surveyor Verplanck Colvin (1847–1920) loved the Adirondacks and was among the first to call for the region's protection. The need for reliable maps and concerns about the impact of unregulated logging on New York's forests and waterways led Colvin to become the State's first Superintendent of the Adirondack Survey in 1872. Traveling mostly by boat and on foot, Colvin created the first reliable maps of this rugged landscape. Vivid written descriptions of his travels through the Adirondack Mountains, published in official reports, read like adventure stories, and brought the region to life for New Yorkers curious about this isolated region.

Verplanck Colvin, *Adirondack Survey, A Preliminary Reconnaissance Sketch*, 1873 (detail).

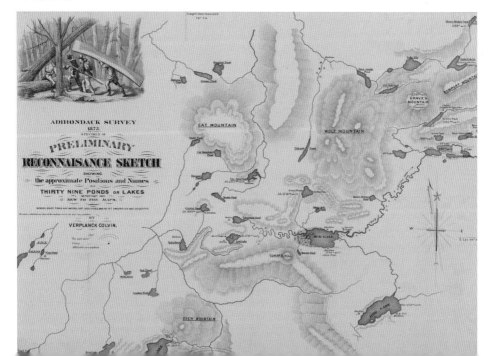

Charles Cromwell Ingham, *The Great Adirondack Pass*, 1837.

Artists discovered the beauty of the Adirondack Mountains even earlier than Colvin, inspired by the seemingly untouched wilderness that extended for miles in all directions. They brought their sketchbooks and fishing poles, following their guides into the High Peaks and uncharted terrain. Many artists still live and work in the Adirondacks. Their paintings are a changing portrait of the Adirondack landscape over time, and reflect the fascination we have with its mountains and waterways.

Levi Wells Prentice, *Near Saranac Lake, Adirondacks*, 1874, oil on canvas.

< Hugh Antoine Fisher, *Rapids of the Ausable*, c. 1910, (detail), watercolor and gouache.

Seneca Ray Stoddard,
*Down Partridge
Hill, Keene Valley,
Adirondacks*, 1890.

Mining, logging, and railroad building also brought
people to the Adirondacks. Successive waves of
immigration provided the manpower needed in these
industries beginning in the nineteenth century,
further opening up the region to travel. Tourists and
sportsmen came as well, inspired by William Henry
Harrison "Adirondack" Murray (1840–1904), a
Boston minister, outdoorsman, writer, and lecturer.
He urged Americans to renew their health and vigor
in the Adirondack Mountains in his 1869 best-selling
book, *Adventures in the Wilderness* or *Camp Life in the
Adirondacks*. Reprinted multiple times, it ignited a
tourism rush in 1870. The region's rustic accommo-
dations, insects, and rain proved daunting to many
under-prepared would-be adventurers derisively
called "Murray's fools" in the press. Most, however,
cherished what they found, and tourism soon
became—and remains—central to Adirondack life.

Bob Marshall, Herb Clark, and George
Marshall, the first 'forty-sixers,' c. 1915.

Exterior of the *Oriental*.

Ford Model T touring car, 1921.

Interior of the *Oriental*, private rail car. >

14

"From a grain of sand to a great mountain, all is sacred."

—Peter Blue Cloud (1935–2011), Mohawk writer

A PEOPLED WILDERNESS:
Native People of the Adirondacks

D. S. Brush, Mitchel Sabattis, c. 1880. Mitchel Sabattis (1821–1906) was one of the most admired and sought-after guides in the Adirondacks. An Abenaki, Sabattis was born in Parishville, but lived his adult life in Long Lake, New York.

A Map of that Part of America which was the Principal Seat of the War in 1756, 1757 (detail).

"Wilderness" suggests land untouched by humans, yet Native Americans have lived within the boundaries of the Adirondack Park for more than 12,000 years. Ancient tools may be found at still-popular campsites and modern roads follow age-old hunting trails. Native people did not draw crisp lines on maps, or place signs along boundaries. Like the air, land could not be owned by an individual or nation, though it was vital to all. Conflicts did occur, but the lightly populated Adirondacks were home to Mohawk, Abenaki, and other Native people for generations.

The Mohawk (Kanienkehaka, or People of the Flint) are the easternmost of the Iroquois Confederacy's six nations. Their ancestral land reaches from the Mohawk Valley north to the St. Lawrence River, covering much of the Adirondacks.

Many Mohawk today live just north of the Adirondack Park on the St. Regis Mohawk Reservation. Known by its Mohawk name, *Akwesasne* (Where the Grouse Drums its Wings), the reservation bridges the borders of New York, Quebec, and Ontario.

The Abenaki (*W8banaki* or People of the Dawn Land) homelands cover much of New England and southern Quebec. As European settlement expanded in New England in the 1600s, Abenaki families shifted westward, reaching as far as Blue Mountain Lake in the late 1700s. Many made the Adirondacks their permanent home. Today, Abenaki people are spread across New York and New England, as well as Odanak, Quebec, seat of the Abenaki government.

Mohawk and Abenaki stories are complex, often misrepresented, and entwined with those of later European arrivals. They lived throughout what is now the Adirondack Park, moving their settlements seasonally or as local resources were depleted. Hunting, fishing, and gathering native plants for food and medicinal purposes were year-round activities here. Although much of their communities today are centered on reservations to the north, the Mohawk and Abenaki never left the Park, and still consider the Adirondack Mountains home.

Today, whether scientists or artists, lumberjacks or historians, the descendants of the Adirondack's original inhabitants remain a powerful influence shaping Adirondack life.

Babe and Carla Hemlock, *So Be It Our Minds*, c. 2016. The Hemlocks are members of the Kahnawake Mohawk community near Montreal. Carla is a textile artist, and Babe is a wood carver and painter. Haudenosaunee-style cradle boards often appear in their work, honoring tradition while looking toward the future.

Henry Arquette (Mohawk), packbasket, 1998. Basket-making is an important part of Native culture, a skill passed down from one generation to the next. Utilitarian work baskets and decorative "fancy baskets" made for the tourist trade are woven from thin strips of wood from the threatened black ash tree.

Mrs. Garvan's Bedroom, Kamp Kill Kare, c. 1915.

Seneca Ray Stoddard, *William West Durant at Great Camp Pine Knot*, c. 1890.

Punch bowl, c. 1880.

ROUGHING IT:
Living in the Wilderness

A fresh start. A break from the ordinary. A chance to reconnect with the land. The rugged Adirondack lifestyle is famously invigorating and revitalizing.

But what does "roughing it" actually mean? Hermits, farmers, and owners of large Great Camp compounds have all had their own definitions.

Living in the Adirondack Park can mean dealing with isolation and the often harsh realities of the Adirondack climate. Native peoples developed shelters and homes using materials found at hand; later European settlers did the same, using timber cut from the surrounding forest.

Early Adirondack visitors relied on the hospitality of residents who opened their homes to travelers. As stagecoaches, railroads, and automobiles brought even more tourists, hotels and cottages appeared, and old ones evolved to attract new clientele. As tourism grew, a few lavish hotels were established, boasting custom china, tennis courts, and full orchestras in the evening. Whether simple or opulent, Adirondack lodgings offered comfort in the "wilderness."

Seneca Ray Stoddard, *Dining room, Hotel Champlain*, 1890.

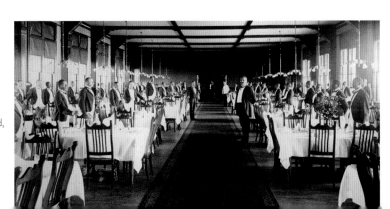

Trudeau Sanitarium, 1892.

As the country became more urbanized, the ills of city living—overcrowding, heat, polluted air and water—led to a major health crisis. Tuberculosis brought thousands to the Adirondacks seeking relief, and maybe a cure, in the balsam-scented mountain air. Dr. Edward Livingston Trudeau (1848–1915) founded the Adirondack Cottage Sanitarium in Saranac Lake in 1884. Nourishing food and bed rest in the open air year-round helped many recover at "the San," which soon had more applicants than beds. Many Saranac Lake homes still feature "cure porches," where patients rested, bundled up against winter's chill.

West of the Wind, built 1965, in *Life in the Adirondacks*.

Wealthy urbanites sought relief from the summer heat, building large, rustic compounds called Great Camps in the Adirondack woods that featured all the comforts of home. But beginning in the twentieth century, some chose to live more simply, without modern amenities. Scientist, writer, guide, photographer, and conservationist Anne LaBastille (1933–2011) moved to Twitchell Lake in 1965, building a waterfront log cabin with no electricity, running water, or road access. There she found the solitude she needed to write her widely-read autobiographies: the Woodswoman series, published between 1976 and 2003. As both a writer and mentor, LaBastille encouraged like-minded women to live and work close to nature and to take an active role in the conservation movement.

Anne LaBastille on the steps of her cabin, c. 1980.

Nancie Battaglia, Prospect Point Cottages, Blue Mountain Lake. >

22

George Baldwin, Abbott Augustus Low, 1901.
Maple sap was, and in many places still is, collected in galvanized metal buckets. A. A. Low, owner of Horseshoe Forestry Company, checks maple sap collection on his property in the Town of Piercefield, New York.

ADIRONDACK TOUGH:
Work in the Wilderness

For centuries, the rhythm of work in the Adirondacks was closely tied to the land. Seasonal tasks like growing and gathering food, collecting maple sap to make syrup and sugar, and clearing roads of snow are all part of life in the Adirondacks to this day. Although industries like mining and logging were once major employers in the Adirondack Park, most residents no longer work directly with the land.

Logging was the first big money-making industry in the Adirondacks. In the 1850s, the region was the leading timber producer in the country. By 1885, about one-third of forested areas inside the Blue Line had been cleared. Soft woods like spruce, which float, were cut and sent downriver to sawmills and market. Charcoal, used as fuel for the forges processing Adirondack iron ore, required large amounts of hardwood and resulted in nearly 5,000 acres of clear-cut every year. Concerns about the impact of deforestation resulted in the creation of the Forest Preserve in 1885 and ultimately the Adirondack Park in 1892. Mechanization in the last century greatly reduced the workforce required in logging, and large forestry companies, faced with declining markets, sold large tracts of land to the state in the early twenty-first century. Although it no longer employs the large numbers of people it once did, logging is still part of the Adirondack economy.

Cutting ice, Blue Mountain Lake, 1958.
Charles Arnold of North Creek, New York, modified a 1929 Chevrolet 6-cylinder engine to make this pond—or ice—saw. Used on Blue Mountain, Utowana, and Eagle Lakes, it was capable of cutting as many as 1800 blocks of ice a day, supplying area camps and hotels with refrigeration for perishable foods.

Load of logs from Red Dog Mountain, 1899.

Five ores and minerals have been mined inside the Blue Line: iron, titanium, graphite, wollastonite, and garnet. The discovery of magnetite, a magnetic iron ore, made the Adirondacks a major producer of wrought- and cast-iron during the nineteenth century. Graphite found in the Ticonderoga area was used to make pencils and industrial crucibles. Titanium, once considered an impurity in Adirondack iron ore, was mined in Tahawus, near Newcomb, during World War II.

The success or failure of any mining operation has always been determined by global supply and demand. Although the region still contains large amounts of high-quality ores, particularly iron and titanium, much of it lies thousands of feet below ground. After World War II, the costs of extracting these ores from such depths became too great.

John "Shorty" Deresky, Mineville, 1951.

Miners, 13th Lake Mine, c. 1900.

The Don B Shaft, Moriah, New York, c. 1960.

MINING MOUNTAINS

THE ADIRONDACK GEOLOGIC DOME was pushed up when two contino...
billion years ago. Younger rocks weathered away, exposing ancient, deep-...
from ocean sediments and lava. Hidden in this rock were pockets of rare a...

Graphite, iron and tit...   ...ce mined here, and two ores are m...
Adirondack Park tod...   ...orth River, and wollastonite in Lewis a...
Both minerals are fou...   ...s outside the Adirondacks, which giv...
a competitive edge.

Meet a
MINER

ADIRONDACK
IRON

AS EARLY AS THE 1700S, IRON MINING SHAPED THE LANDSCAPE AND CHARACTER of many Adirondack communities. Mines and bloomery forges once dotted the landscape and mining towns grew around them. Nearby forests were leveled, turned into charcoal to feed forges.

By 1900, locals here had been joined by waves of immigrants. Many mining towns were made up of small ethnic communities of Eastern and Western European immigrants and African Americans who moved north to escape the segregated South in the 20th century. It was hard, dangerous work that helped build the America we know.

DANGER

BLASTING
IN PROGRESS

HIGH EXPLOSIVES
DANGEROUS

Matthias Oppersdorf, *James A. LaTour*, 1986–87.

Matthias Oppersdorf, *Henry Kashiwa*, 1986–87.

Eliot Porter, *Beaver Meadow Falls with Leaves*, 1965.

Less expensive ores extracted in open pits in the American West, India, South Africa, and Brazil forced widespread mine closures in the Adirondacks. Beginning in the late twentieth century, large, corporate mining operations in the Adirondack region began to pull out.

Although mining has largely disappeared from the region, there are still working mines: in North River, industrial-grade garnet used for cutting and polishing is extracted; and in Willsboro, wollastonite, a fibrous mineral used as an insulating and strengthening agent, is still mined.

Today, only three percent of the Adirondack Park's workforce is employed in agriculture, mining, or forestry. The vast majority of the Park's 133,000 residents work in government, service industries like medicine and education, or in sales and food service. As it has been since the late nineteenth century, tourism is the Adirondack's largest industry today, a seasonal industry closely tied to the region's landscape, climate, and scenery.

"It is impossible for those who have not visited this region to realize the abundance, luxuriance and depth which these peaty mosses—the true source of our rivers— attain under the shade of those dark northern evergreen forests... The remedy for this is an Adirondack park or timber preserve." —Verplanck Colvin, c. 1868

OUR ADIRONDACK PARK

Whiteface Mountain Fire Tower, 1935.

The largest, and most important, artifact the **Adirondack Experience** interprets is the landscape that surrounds the museum—the Adirondack Park itself. The Park is both a historical document and a living vision of the world we will leave to our children and grand-children. The natural world is a community to which we all belong and nowhere is this more consciously recognized than in the Adirondack Park—one of the oldest conservation experiments in the world. The Park is a model of how humans and nature can coexist to mutual benefit, and how sustainable activities and human prosperity can go hand-in-hand.

The Adirondack Park's six million acres cover 9,375 square miles, traditionally outlined on maps with a blue line. Within the Park's Blue Line are both public and private lands: approximately 2.5 million acres are pro-tected public land; 3.5 million acres are privately owned. It is this combination that makes the Park unique.

The Adirondack Park Agency (APA) is the state agency created in 1971 to protect and preserve the private and public lands within the "Blue Line," enforcing development and land use regulations.

< Nancie Battaglia, aerial view of Blue Mountain Lake and the **Adirondack Experience**.

Their charge requires agency staff to "seek a balance of conservation, protection, preservation, development, and use of the resources of the Adirondack Park." In addition to government regulations, private organizations also work to preserve both working and wild landscapes. The Nature Conservancy, the Adirondack Land Trust, and private landowners are taking steps to ensure the preservation of wild forests, farms, timberlands, and shorelines.

Nancie Battaglia, Blue Mountain Lake from The Hedges.

Scientists have studied the Adirondack environment since geologist Ebenezer Emmons first explored the region in the 1830s. The lessons learned here have global implications. Today, Rensselaer Polytechnic Institute, IBM, and The FUND for Lake George are working together on The Jefferson Project: an innovative partnership that develops and deploys new sensor technology, experiments, and computer models to better understand the effects of weather, climate, and human activities on Lake George and guide decisions about its future. This work may one day be used worldwide to assess and protect freshwater and marine ecosystems and the people who rely on them.

Throughout its history, the people who live, work, and play in the Adirondack Park have endeavored to care for it. In spite of the diversity of opinions about how to do so, this is a success story: even as we struggle with a growing population and environmental problems, this place serves as a model for how humans and nature may coexist to mutual benefit, and how sustainable activities and human prosperity need not be mutually exclusive.

"The Closet," 1957. Although the Adirondack Park was created for public benefit, not everyone was always equally welcome here. This small addition was built to house the Seagle Music Colony's first African American student in 1957 as the alternative to boarding him with white students.

Nancie Battaglia, sailboat on Blue Mountain Lake. >

32

WOODS AND WATERS:
Outdoor Recreation in the Adirondacks

J. J. Rondeau
Adirondack
Hermit.

"**Whither shall we flee from civilization, to take off the harness and ties of society, and rest for a season, from the restraints, the conventionalities of society... the strifes and competitions of life?**" —Lawyer, author, and politician Samuel H. Hammond, 1857

Arthur Fitzwilliam Tait, *A Good Time Coming*, 1862, oil on canvas.

Seneca Ray Stoddard, *Col. E. A. McAlpin and Guide*, c. 1890.

To Native Americans, all of nature was meaningful and life-sustaining. They made no distinction between "wilderness" and the rest of creation. To the first European Americans, the wilderness seemed a hostile, devilish place, the antithesis of Christian civilization. Not until the nineteenth century did the idea of unspoiled nature appeal to Americans skeptical about the dizzying pace of progress and technology.

Between 1800 and 1900, the United States shifted from an agricultural to a largely urban, industrial, and commercial society. During this time of great change, the Adirondacks became one of the nation's sacred places. In an age of ruthless exploitation of the American landscape, with dramatic changes in patterns of life and work, the Adirondacks came to represent a return to redemptive and unspoiled nature. For Americans stressed by increasingly fast-paced, often desk-bound lives, the Adirondack wilderness was a recreational paradise where trout, deer, unpolluted air and water, and healthy exercise could restore

< Noah John Rondeau, 1978.

Frederick Sackrider Remington, *Untitled (Ab Thompson's Cabin on Silver Lake)*, c. 1890, oil on canvas.

body and spirit. The roots of the American love for wilderness and the origins of the American camping trip are here in the Adirondacks, the nation's first great wilderness destination.

While some of clergyman William Murray's parishioners found his passion for outdoor life rough and unseemly, he advocated outdoor sports as a means of restoring men to health and a closer relationship to God. His brand of "muscular Christianity" found a ready audience in those who, "pent up in narrow offices and narrower studies, weary of the city's din, long for a breath of mountain air and the free life by field and flood." When his *Adventures in the Wilderness...* was published in 1869, he intended it as a guide to outdoor recreation in the Adirondacks, but the book was criticized for glossing over the difficulties of getting by in the woods, and for inspiring thousands of inexperienced sportsmen and women (the aforementioned "Murray's fools") to head into the wilderness. Nevertheless, public interest in outdoor life continued to grow, and for the first time, people began camping out as a recreational activity.

Matthias Oppersdorf, *Gary Hodgson*, 1986–87. Hodgson was a Forest Ranger and member of the New York State Helicopter Rescue Team.

Nancie Battaglia, hikers descending Blue Mountain in November snow. >

Car camping, c. 1950.

MARION RIVER CARRY PAVILION

Seneca Ray Stoddard, *The Stella on Raquette Lake*, c. 1885.

Porter Engine from the Marion River Carry, 1900.

Killoquah, at Marion River Carry, c. 1890.

Osprey, c. 1900.

In 1899, William West Durant (1850–1934) built a rail line over the Marion River Carry at the west end of Utowana Lake in the central Adirondacks. A carry, or portage, is a route over land between two bodies of water. Once the shortest standard-gauge railroad in the world at three-quarters of a mile long, it featured three horse-drawn passenger cars discarded by the Brooklyn Rapid Transit Company and a light locomotive built by the H. K. Porter Company in Pittsburgh. Until the train went out of service in 1929, it carried between 8,000 and 10,000 passengers (and their baggage) each year from the Raquette River to steamboats on the Eckford Chain. The boats made stops at hotels and other destinations on Utowana, Eagle, and Blue Mountain Lakes. The Porter engine and one of the passenger cars were installed on the grounds in 1955, two years before the museum opened.

The *Osprey* is a small steam-powered launch built by Charles W. Durant, Jr., in 1882. The wooden hull was probably made in the Adirondacks; the engine was built by Clute Brothers & Company in Schenectady, New York. Originally called the *Stella*, the boat was renamed by her second owner, J. Harvey Ladew, in the late 1880s. Although the *Osprey* is typical of the steamboats that shuttled passengers on the Eckford Chain, she was used as a private conveyance in Raquette Lake.

WORK IN THE WOODS:
Logging the Adirondacks

"An industrious chopper will cut from fifty to sixty logs a day, while an expert axman under favorable conditions will have cut one hundred logs in a day. The number of logs cut makes some difference in the pay... Thus the rate of lumbermen's wages from $25 to $40 per month, and board." —Lee J. Vance, 1896

Logging was once one of New York's—and the Adirondack's—major industries. It was the primary employer in such towns as Tupper Lake, Newcomb, Conifer, Lyons Falls, Poland, Watertown, Carthage, Potsdam, Glens Falls, Fulton, Hudson Falls, and many more. As late as 1950 some Adirondack towns still depended on turning wood into useful products. Logging in the Adirondacks is a history of men, machines, and the changes that transformed the early woodsman from a man with an axe, cross-cut saw, and a horse to an industrial worker wearing a hard hat and armed with an array of machinery.

By 1850, America's forested areas had become greatly diminished. The Adirondack forest was one of the last in the Northeast to be logged. The region's mountains, cold winters, and sparse population hindered timber harvesting until later in the nineteenth century. Logging activity grew when the railroads arrived in the 1890s and large sawmills and paper mills were built within the Park.

Adirondack lumberjacks came from varied backgrounds: English, French-Canadian, Irish, Scotch-Irish, Italian, Scandinavian, German, Polish, Lithuanian, and Russian. Work was hard, amenities few, accidents frequent, pay minimal, and hours long. They went into the woods in the fall and did not reemerge until spring.

Logging was highly labor intensive, but that changed beginning in the early twentieth century. Power-driven machinery replaced men and horses as the principal means of harvesting. Mechanization—

Log load near Tupper Lake, c. 1915.

Meal time in a logging camp, c. 1900. Lumber camp cooks worked seven days a week for many months at a time, often putting in longer days than the lumberjacks.

Utley Bros., *Accident at Pullman's Mill, June 14th, 1906*, lithograph. In 1906, George Lanz was operating an edging machine when it malfunctioned, forcing a 14-foot by 4-inch piece of wood into his back, pinning his right arm to his side. He recovered and returned to work at the Turner mill in Derrick.

44

River driver standing on a log, c. 1900.

Stephen Story, *The Loader near Charlie Pond, Adirondacks, N.Y.*, 1982, oil on canvas.

< Richard J. Linke, *Loading logs in Newcomb*, 1973–74.

chainsaws for cutting, tractors for skidding, trucks for hauling—changed logging from a seasonal occupation into a year-round operation. Now, with specialized equipment like feller bunchers and self-loading trucks, only small crews of men are needed.

Adirondack forests produce two sorts of commercial logs: saw and pulp. Saw logs, which are high-quality wood, become lumber and furniture. Most Adirondack logs are pulp logs, which become paper and biomass. To have a healthy forest economy you must have local processors who will buy both.

In forestry, as in farming, the profits go to the processors, not the producers. Relatively little money is made by growing trees or cutting them. Substantially more is made by turning them into lumber, furniture, paper, or energy. By this standard, the Adirondack forest economy is not very healthy. Although there are a number of mills in outlying areas, including southeastern Canada, there are no longer large mills operating within the Park.

Adirondack pulpwood has gained new importance as biomass, a source of renewable energy. A growing number of regional electric-generating plants and other industrial and institutional facilities have converted to burning wood chips and grindings for fuel. There is an increasing demand for pulpwood to produce wood pellets and compacted sawdust for use in homes and businesses. Wood has also shown promise as a source of liquid biofuel and for producing industrial chemicals.

BOATS AND BOATING
IN THE ADIRONDACKS

> **"It should be remembered that in this 'Venice of America' nearly all the traveling is done by means of boats."**
> —Guidebook publisher E. R. Wallace, 1895

Before the advent of the automobile, the Adirondack's 3,000 lakes and ponds and 30,000 miles of rivers and streams were the region's highways. Boats were essential to life in this rugged, mountainous area.

The dugout and birchbark canoe are the oldest forms of watercraft used in the Adirondacks. Made from hollowed-out tree trunks, heavy dugouts were used by the Iroquois on larger lakes where there was no need to carry the boat over land. Canoes made of tough, flexible birchbark are lightweight, portable, and easier to use when traveling across one of the many Adirondack carries (portages) between bodies of water. By the nineteenth century, the bark canoe was also used by European settlers and sportsmen, but other boats were becoming more common on Adirondack waters.

The guideboat is a small wooden craft that evolved in the Adirondacks beginning in the early nineteenth century from skiffs used for hunting and fishing. Light enough for one person to carry, it can bear large, heavy loads making it an ideal work boat. With a long narrow bottom board the guideboat can be rather unstable but fast. Each end of the boat is higher than the middle, which helps keep it dry in rough water. Once the workhorse of the region, these widely recognized boats are now primarily used for pleasure.

As railroads and better roads brought increasing numbers of tourists, all types of canoes, rowing boats, and mechanically powered boats appeared. Steamboats carried tourists from stagecoach stops and railroad depots to hotels as early as 1824 on Lake George.

Seneca Ray Stoddard, *View from the Stern Seat*, 1888.

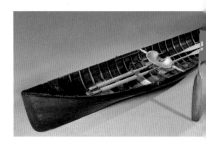

Guideboat, 1890–1910.

Willard and Paulina Hanmer in a boat shop, Saranac Lake, 1961.

Boat builder Allison Warner puts the finishing touches on a guideboat. >

Henry M. Beach, *The Marion River*, c. 1910.

By the 1870s, even smaller bodies of water in the Adirondack interior boasted regular steamboat service, delivering mail and offering excursions as well as transportation. Naphtha and electric launches were popular at the end of the nineteenth century among the well-to-do, but were quickly eclipsed with the advent of the internal combustion engine.

By the early twentieth century, gasoline-powered marine engines were reliable and inexpensive enough to come into popular use. Clubs of motorboat enthusiasts sponsored social gatherings and races, celebrating and testing the speed of the latest engine models. Racing boats, built purely for speed, found a home on Lake George, site of several Gold Cup races in the teens and 1930s. George Reis' *El Lagarto*, the "Leaping Lizard of Lake George," won three consecutive Gold Cup victories, once reaching the unheard-of seventy-two miles-per-hour on a straightaway. Nurse Anne Jenson raced *Go for Broke* all over the Adirondacks, including Schroon Lake, where she and her husband had a summer home.

Speedboat racing, 1969.

During the Great Depression, fewer people could indulge in such luxuries as a boat. After World War II, as the national economy recovered, there was a resurgence in pleasure boating and interest in traditional, wooden craft. Today people use a wide variety of watercraft in the Adirondacks, including kayaks, canoes, small sailboats, pontoons, and fishing boats. There are still guideboat builders working here, building their boats with wood in the traditional manner, or using more modern materials like Kevlar.

Nancie Battaglia, paddlers heading out on Blue Mountain Lake from Hemlock Hall.

< Photograph by Nancie Battaglia.

THE LOG HOTEL:
Merwin's Blue Mountain House

"**Wanderers are we in search of the beautiful, as, with our backs to the dusty city and our faces set toward the mountains, we move swiftly along.**"

—Seneca Ray Stoddard, *Lake George: (Illustrated) A Book of Today*, 1880

The Log Hotel was built in 1876 by Miles Tyler Merwin, early settler and lumberman, as his home. In 1880, he built a large frame hotel, the Blue Mountain House, with a broad verandah overlooking the lake. The Log Hotel became additional guest quarters, with two small cabins added by the 1880s. A stamp found on several of the Log Hotel's hand-hewn spruce logs indicates that the wood was harvested and sold by R. M. Hawkins of Glens Falls.

By 1907, the Blue Mountain House hotel could accommodate as many as a hundred guests. True to his Methodist background, Merwin banned the use of alcohol and tobacco on hotel grounds, although he did offer amusements including "ping-pong, piano, Victrola, radio, and when occasion demands, square and regular dancing."

In 1935 Merwin retired, selling the hotel to William Wessels. Times were changing, however, and the days of the grand Adirondack hotels were over. The automobile changed the way Americans vacationed. Most preferred to travel by car rather than train, and to stay at smaller, less expensive motels and tourist camps. In the Adirondacks, large luxury hotels found it difficult to compete for guests. In 1954, Wessels sold the hotel to the newly-formed Adirondack Historical Association.

The Log Hotel, built in 1876.

Brochures for Blue Mountain House, 1940s.

Blue Mountain House and Cottages and Lake, c. 1890.

BLUE MOUNTAIN HOUSE AND COTTAGES AND LAKE. (From hill in rear of house.)

56

Opening Day, August 4, 1957.

The Porter Engine, Marion River Carry Pavilion, 1957.

The Adirondack Museum, 1957.

Sunset Cottage, c. 1880. Sunset Cottage is one of the finest surviving examples of mosaic twig design in the Adirondacks. Built at Camp Cedars, on Forked Lake, as a place for guests to change before swimming, it originally featured a wraparound porch on all sides. It was salvaged and moved across the ice by owner C. V. Whitney after the blowdown of 1950 destroyed the camp and later donated to the museum.

A NEW MUSEUM

On August 4, 1957, the Adirondack Museum opened to the public. Built on the site of the Blue Mountain House, a new exhibition hall replaced the aging hotel, mirroring its horseshoe footprint. The new building was state-of-the art, featuring audio recordings and a motorized "photo belt," a conveyor belt with copies of photographs from the collection that moved past the seated visitor. Five hundred visitors came on opening day to see these and the old Porter Engine and railcar that once moved passengers and luggage over the Marion River Carry.

In the decades since, the museum has grown to twenty-three buildings, with 65,000 square feet of exhibition space. The 121-acre museum campus features buildings like Sunset Cottage and Buck Lake Club, historic structures moved here from around the Adirondack Park; a pond stocked with native trout; an authentic schoolhouse and play area; outdoor sculptures; a combination of wild and manicured

Marion River Carry Pavilion.

grounds and gardens; and a hiking trail and boathouse on Minnow Pond.

The Minnow Pond Trail dates from the late nineteenth century and is "a delightful walk, all on the level, through the forest to a gem in the wilderness." Along this and similar trails throughout the Adirondacks, hikers and paddlers access thousands of lakes and endless miles of rivers. Today, the Minnow Pond Trail offers a new entry point for Adirondack paddlers. From a turn-of-the-twentieth century Rushton guideboat to contemporary rowboats, visitors can walk the trail to the ADKX Boathouse, rent a boat, and explore the serenity of Minnow Pond.

In 2017, we celebrated our sixtieth anniversary year with a new name: **Adirondack Experience: The Museum on Blue Mountain Lake.** Our new identity reflects the transformation of the museum into a rich interactive experience, a social space that encourages the creation of shared, lasting memories in an indoor-outdoor environment. The 19,000-square-foot-exhibition *Life in the Adirondacks* combines authentic artifacts with technology, immersing visitors in the spirit of adventure to bring the Adirondack experience to life.

Minnow Pond Trail.

ADIRONDACK EXPERIENCE™
The Museum on Blue Mountain Lake

Our new logo combines the letters A (Adirondack) and X (Experience) in an abstract image that evokes the High Peaks and rustic Adirondack architecture. Reflecting both the indoor and outdoor aspects of the museum, the logo communicates our continuous exploration into the history and beauty of life in the Adirondacks.

58

GENERAL INFORMATION

OPEN SEASON

The ADKX is open from Memorial Day Weekend to mid-October.

LAKE VIEW CAFÉ AND OUTDOOR PICNIC AREAS

Take a break from exploring the grounds and enjoy a spectacular panorama of Blue Mountain Lake. The Lake View Café is open from 10 a.m. to 4 p.m. and offers hot and cold dishes, snacks, and beverages. Visitors who wish to experience lunch in the great outdoors can take advantage of the picnic areas scattered across the grounds that can accommodate group and individual picnics. Each area includes trash receptacles and recycling centers, which all visitors are encouraged to use to help keep our campus pristine.

Photograph by Nancie Battaglia.

COLLECTIONS

Adirondack Experience has been collecting and interpreting objects that represent the lives of Adirondack visitors and residents for more than sixty years. The stories these objects tell form a rich documentary of the ways people have understood and interacted with the environment of the Adirondack Park. These are stories that touch on our innate need to connect with nature, our struggle to survive and adapt to a changing environment and, ultimately, lessons in balancing the needs of human communities with the natural world. Although the stories we tell are Adirondack, they have meaning and relevance for people around the world. *The collections are available to researchers by appointment.*

LIBRARY

The **Adirondack Experience Library** is the largest, most comprehensive repository of books, ephemera, manuscripts, maps, and government documents relating to the history of the Adirondack region. The library-of-record for the Adirondack Park, it collects, preserves, and organizes all forms of information related to the region, and shares that information with genealogists, writers, historians, students, and anyone with an interest in the Adirondacks. *The library is open to researchers by appointment Monday through Friday from 8:30 a.m. to 4:30 p.m.*

Nancie Battaglia, vendors at the **Adirondack Experience** Rustic Fair.

SPECIAL EVENTS AND PROGRAMS

All season long, the **Adirondack Experience** hosts a full calendar of events, from live music to lectures, special presentations, artisans-in-residence, demonstrations, workshops, rustic furniture fairs, antique shows, and more. All special events (with the exception of the Antiques Early Buying Event) are included with general admission.

CHANGING EXHIBITIONS

The **Adirondack Experience** offers special changing exhibitions of art, history, and culture that showcase our rich collections and take an in-depth look at an Adirondack topic.

STORE

Unique local and global items from past and present. Find something for every occasion and age group! Explore the ADKX Store at the **Adirondack Experience: The Museum on Blue Mountain Lake**; or at **www.theadkxstore.com.**

JOIN AND SUPPORT

The **Adirondack Experience** depends on financial support through membership, donations to the Annual Fund, special programs, and exhibits. We invite you to play a key role in keeping our exhibits fresh and vibrant, our programs thoughtful and entertaining, our outreach efforts ongoing, and securing our next fifty years. Every gift makes a difference.

Membership in the **Adirondack Experience** includes free admission, along with several other members-only privileges. What's more, your support plays an important role in helping us to continue to share the beauty and history of the Adirondacks that we all love.

OUR MISSION

The **Adirondack Experience** expands public understanding of Adirondack history and the relationship between people and the Adirondack wilderness, fostering informed choices for the future.

Below left and right: Nancie Battaglia, ADKX Store and Visitors' Center.